Advance Praise for Mind

"*Mindful with Me* offers proven, practical, and fun practices for integrating mindfulness into our family lives. Another wonderful and unique addition to family practice." —Chris Willard, PsyD, Harvard Medical School faculty, author of *Growing Up Mindful: Essential Practices to Help Children, Teens, and Families Find Balance, Calm, and Resilience*

"*Mindful with Me* is packed with practical techniques and playful activities that empower children and their grown-ups to find calm and regulation by embracing the present. This easy-to-use book offers parents, teachers, and caregivers invaluable tools to nurture children's emotional and mental health. Everyday moments become mindful opportunities, building a foundation for a lifetime of well-being." —Kira Willey, musician and author of *Breathe Like a Bear: 30 Mindful Moments for Kids to Feel Calm and Focused Anytime, Anywhere*

"As parents, we all want to be connected with our children. We all want to notice and savor the beautiful moments. In *Mindful with Me*, Sarah Dennehy makes connecting not just possible, but easy and fun. Packed with dozens of evidence-based, kid-friendly practices, *Mindful with Me* shows us how to deeply enhance our own lives and those of our children with mindfulness." —Shonda Moralis, MSW, LCSW, author of *Breathe, Mama, Breathe: 5-Minute Mindfulness for Busy Moms*

MINDFUL
WITH ME

MiNDFUL WITH ME

Connecting with Your Child through Daily Mindfulness

SARAH DENNEHY, M.Ed.

ILLUSTRATIONS BY NATALIE GARBER MARTIN

THE
collective
BOOK STUDIO

Library of Congress Cataloging-in-Publication Data available.

ISBN: 978-1-68555-678-5

Ebook ISBN: 978-1-68555-385-2

Library of Congress Control Number: 2023919443

Printed using Forest Stewardship Council certified stock from sustainably managed forests.

Manufactured in China.

Design by Carole Chevalier.

10 9 8 7 6 5 4 3 2 1

The Collective Book Studio®

Oakland, California

www.thecollectivebook.studio

For Jack and Isla

I invite you to pause . . .

✳

Soften your shoulders, your jaw, and the
space between your eyebrows.

✳

Feel the support of the chair or ground
beneath you.

✳

Breathe in slowly . . . and breathe out
even more slowly.

And just *be* for a moment.

CONTENTS

INTRODUCTION

Welcome.

I wrote *Mindful with Me* to help parents and children connect through mindfulness. Whether you already have a mindfulness practice or you're brand new to the concept, you're in the right place, and I'm so glad you're here.

In my years working with families as a behavioral consultant, I have witnessed firsthand how many parents and children rush through their days, trying to do everything on their schedule, yet frequently too busy and exhausted to spend (much-needed) quality time together. These families—who are just trying to keep up with the daily demands of life—are often stressed out, feel overwhelmed, and wish they had more time to connect with each other. When I later became certified to teach children's mindfulness, it became clear to me that mindfulness is an effective and enjoyable bridge for families—a simple way to help parents and children connect. At the same time, mindfulness offers a range of practical and health benefits, including teaching valuable behavioral, physical, mental, and emotional skills.

I developed the framework of *Mindful with Me* as a way for you (and caregivers, teachers, or anyone who lives or works with children) to teach mindfulness strategies and skills to your child. Practicing mindfulness together just minutes a day can help your child better self-regulate and work through big feelings. In these intentional moments, you can also develop your own mindfulness skills and self-awareness—all while building deep connections with your child.

To help you integrate mindfulness seamlessly into your day, this book contains fun activities and inspiring practice ideas, laid out in a simple, easy-to-follow manner.

What Is Mindfulness, Exactly?

As a children's mindfulness teacher, I often get blank stares when I tell people what I do. And I get it—the concept of mindfulness can be a bit ambiguous.

Years ago, when I began my meditation practice, I'd heard the word *mindfulness*, but didn't quite know what it meant. I assumed it was interchangeable with the word *meditation*. It wasn't until a few years later, when I decided to pursue a children's yoga and mindfulness certification, that I discovered that mindfulness is more than just sitting in stillness.

Mindfulness is paying attention to the present moment with curiosity and kindness. It sounds straightforward enough—you're paying attention and you're doing it through a lens of compassion. But what does that really mean? Are we supposed to be present each and every waking moment? What does mindfulness actually look like day to day?

Here's what mindfulness means to me:

Mindfulness is pausing to notice the cozy feeling of being indoors on a snowy day. It's the feeling of gratitude as you admire the colors of a sunset. It's recognizing your own physical or mental pain and allowing it to *be* without letting it dictate your next move. It's the sensation of warm water running over your hands and the scent of the soap as you wash a pan after dinner. It's how you treat others and how you respond to difficult situations. It's taking the time to really listen to a friend with an open heart and mind, not just waiting for your turn to speak. It's an awareness of the beauty of simple moments and small joys that are scattered throughout each day, like sunlight patterns on the wall or a deep belly laugh.

In practicing mindfulness with your child, you'll discover your own paths and meanings, along with increased awareness of the joys in day-to-day life.

How Would You Like to Spend Your Days?

Writer Annie Dillard said, "How we spend our days is, of course, how we spend our lives." Many of us are stuck in an ongoing to-do list. There's so much out there competing for our attention that we easily get caught up in the race and tend to forget that our lives are happening right now. We have little control over most things, but we do have control over how we spend our time and where we choose to place our attention.

Mindfulness helps you be intentional about how you spend your days.

When you're spending time with your child and you're fully present, you form deeper connections. In these moments, your child will feel seen, valued, and safe. They know that no matter how they're feeling or what they're experiencing, they can come to you for support and understanding. These mindful connections help support your child's development as a compassionate, self-aware, authentic person.

How to Use This Book

You may be asking yourself if it's possible to not only get your child to sit still long enough to practice mindfulness, but also to want to do it every day. (And it's okay if you don't do it every day. Just aim to do it as consistently as you can.) Establishing an ongoing mindfulness practice with your child may be easier than you think, and this book will walk you through it step by step.

To kick off, the first two chapters will help you establish a foundation and space for your practice. Chapter 1 helps you explore why you would want a mindfulness practice in the first place and how it's beneficial for both you and your child. In chapter 2, I introduce the *connection corner*: the physical space that you and your child will create and use for your daily practice.

Once your foundation is established (and this is important in building a sustainable practice), it's time to dive into the activities, or what you'll be doing in the connection corner. The activities are divided among six chapters: Breathe, Focus, Feel, Care, Rest, and Go.

Each of these chapters features four types of activities:

Let's Pause

Breathing exercises and other activities you can do together either seated or lying down

Let's Connect

Games and activities designed to foster discussion and closeness

Let's Move

Movement-based activities to either energize you or help you wind down, whichever is needed most

Let's Create

Mindful crafts and activities designed to inspire creative minds

Most of the activities (with the exception of some in the Let's Create category) can be completed in five minutes or less.

Chapter 9 will help you put it all together. You'll find suggestions to help you set up your own routines for the connection corner and throughout your whole day.

Over time, as you become more familiar with the activities and strategies covered in this book, you'll find that the connection corner will become portable as well. You'll be able to both practice mindfulness in this space at home and weave a more informal practice throughout your day, no matter where you are.

Personalize Your Practice

Although the activities in this book are suggested for ages four to eight, they can all be easily modified based on your child's age and maturity level. Most of the activities can be done with more than one child at a time and will work just as well in a classroom setting or a therapist's office.

Experiment with the different mindfulness practices to find activities that are meaningful to you and your child. As you work your way through the activities chapters together, I invite you to bookmark or dog-ear pages, write in the margins, star your favorite activities, and make them your own. Within the activities, you'll be invited to sit, stand, dance, or walk. If you or your child has a physical limitation, feel free to modify activities or choose the ones that are most comfortable for you.

As you begin practicing mindfulness with your child, I encourage you to stay curious and present—and above all, have fun.

Let's go!

Chapter 1

INSPIRE

Mindful with Me is about establishing a mindfulness practice that you and your child can do side by side. Before we get started, let's talk a little bit about why you're here.

* Maybe you've been looking for a way to help your child cope with anxiety and the day-to-day challenges of our complicated world.

* Maybe your child has learned about mindfulness at school and has expressed interest in it.

* Maybe you've heard about mindfulness and are wondering if it would be a good fit for your child or yourself.

* Maybe you know nothing about mindfulness or its benefits, but this just looked like a really cool book.

* Or maybe you're thinking, *Well, obviously I'm here because I want to connect with my child through daily mindfulness, just like it says on the cover!*

A consistent mindfulness practice comes with lots of benefits. In this chapter, we'll focus on those benefits to help you discover your *why* and create a solid foundation for the practice you'll share with your child.

Benefits of Mindfulness

As we talked about in the introduction, mindfulness is an awareness of the present moment. It's a way of living intentionally. By focusing on the present moment, mindfulness lets us pause in the space between what's happening and our reaction to it. With the increased sense of awareness that a mindfulness practice brings, we can pause and *decide* how we want to respond. We can make a thoughtful choice, instead of automatically reacting, for example, from a state of panic.

Often, I'll walk into a classroom to lead a mindfulness session and the teacher will say something like, "I'm so glad you're here. We *really* need mindfulness today." In other words, things are feeling a bit hectic here, and we could all use some calm.

Yes, mindfulness can help you feel calm, but there are many other benefits. A consistent mindfulness practice can lead to decreased stress and anxiety, as well as:

* increased emotional regulation and cognitive function
* improved attention and focus
* better sleep
* improved academic performance
* increased self-compassion and empathy
* more connected relationships
* greater self-control

Mindful Research

In the late 1970s, Jon Kabat-Zinn studied using mindfulness to reduce symptoms of chronic pain. Kabat-Zinn described mindfulness as "the awareness that arises from paying attention, on purpose, in the present moment and nonjudgmentally" and showed that a consistent practice of mindfulness meditation could improve mental health in many ways beyond reducing pain. For example, mindfulness can reduce anxiety and depression, and increase self-awareness and self-confidence in adults.

Since then, many research findings have documented how mindfulness also benefits our physical well-being and improves cognitive functioning. More recently, especially within the last fifteen years, there has been an increase in research studies highlighting similar benefits of mindfulness specifically for children, including increases in emotional regulation, focus and attention, and prosocial behaviors.

See Resources for more information about mindfulness research.

Mindfulness as Self-Care

At this point, after reading about all of these benefits, why you're here may feel like a no-brainer. Who wouldn't want all of those things for their child?

Children learn by observing us. When you practice mindfulness, you're modeling for your child that mental and physical health matters. Each time you pause in your day to practice mindfulness, you're practicing self-care.

Self-care was not a priority for many of us growing up, and it may have been viewed as something selfish or frivolous. Subsequently, it's become something we might do when we realize we're super stressed out, instead of something we do each day so we don't *become* super stressed out in the first place. Even if we know we should be practicing self-care consistently, it frequently ends up on the bottom of our to-do list (read: it rarely gets done).

When self-care is one of your priorities, it becomes one of your child's too.

How Does Mindfulness Reduce Stress?

When you experience a stressful event, the sympathetic nervous system kicks in and your body goes into survival mode, commonly known as fight-or-flight. Once the stressful event has passed, the parasympathetic nervous system, or rest-and-digest, switches on and allows you to relax.

Mindful breathing activates the parasympathetic nervous system and sends a signal to the sympathetic nervous system that you are safe. A consistent breathing practice and focused mindfulness activities, like the ones you'll find in this book, strengthen the relaxation response and increase your ability to work through stress.

You're in This Together

Your child won't create a consistent practice on their own or by you simply showing them the activities in this book. If you want your child to practice mindfulness, you'll have to practice it as well.

When you and your child practice mindfulness together, it's an opportunity for the two of you to be fully present and connected. At the same time, they're learning coping strategies—tools that will help them self-regulate when they're struggling with a difficult emotion or stressful situation. So, whenever they feel frustrated, they'll know what to do.

Well, not exactly.

In order for your child to learn to *self-regulate*, you're going to need to *coregulate*.

Understanding Coregulation

Coregulation is a process in which a child develops the ability to self-regulate, or manage complex emotions, through connection with nurturing, caring adults. When your infant is upset, they're not able to express and work through their emotions, so you do it for them. You pick them up and say something like, "Oh, that was a loud sound, and it scared you! I'm here. You're okay." You hold them and rock them, and soon they feel calm and safe.

As your child grows and begins to self-soothe, they still need similar feedback from you. They may now be able to verbalize what happened and how they're feeling, but that doesn't mean they don't need you by their side as they work through it. Just because you've been practicing strategies for them to use when they're upset doesn't mean they are necessarily able to apply these strategies in the moment without your support.

The process of coregulation is ongoing and layered. When your child's nervous system is out of balance, or *dysregulated*, your calm and supportive presence soothes their nervous system. However, coregulation is more than remaining calm when your child is struggling. Coregulation is also a proactive process that develops over the years as you provide a safe, predictable environment in which your child feels seen, heard, and understood. You're essentially telling them: "You've got this, *and* I'm here for you."

Coregulation won't make your child dependent on you forever—they're learning to self-regulate, but it takes time. By practicing mindfulness with your child, you're modeling an effective way to regulate yourself and also teaching them strategies that they can eventually use on their own.

Mindfulness Is Not Magic

The intention of this book is not to help you create a child who is calm and pleasant all the time. Difficult feelings and situations will continue to happen, along with messy meltdowns. Mindfulness will help you, the adult, better navigate these times; and with your support, your child will also begin to connect their feelings and behaviors and learn to respond more and react less.

Back to Your *Why*

We've reviewed the benefits of mindfulness and how helpful it can be for both you and your child, so let's go back to why you're here with this book in your hands.

Take a few moments to become aware of your own reasons why you'd like to begin a mindfulness practice with your child. Grab a notebook or journal and put pen to paper, if you'd like, or just spend a few moments thinking about it. A solid *why* that you can revisit from time to time can help you maintain a consistent practice.

Keeping a journal as you explore mindfulness with your child can increase your own self-awareness and help you recognize how both you and your child are benefiting from the mindful moments you're spending together. Over time, as your mindfulness practice strengthens, you may notice that your initial reasons for beginning it evolve as well.

What's Up Next

An important part of establishing a consistent practice is having a space that both of you will want to spend time in each day. In the next chapter, you and your child will begin creating that special space for your mindfulness practice.

Chapter 2

BEGIN

One of the toughest things about starting a mindfulness practice with your child (or any new habit) is remembering to do it and fitting it into your already busy schedule.

The connection corner will help you create and maintain mindfulness as a habit.

What Is the Connection Corner?

Although you and your child can practice mindfulness anywhere, you're more likely to make it a regular routine if you have a designated practice space set up in your home. I refer to this space as the *connection corner*, but feel free to come up with your own name if there's something that feels more meaningful for the two of you.

To your child, the connection corner may simply feel like special time for the two of you to have fun together. The beautiful part is that they're also:

* learning to make time for self-care

* exploring what helps them feel calm and grounded

* becoming more self-aware and compassionate toward themselves and others

* learning that it's safe to express and work through their difficult emotions

* developing a mindfulness practice that will grow and evolve over time

Essentially, the connection corner focuses on two important principles:

* **Skill building:** When your child is in a calm, regulated state, they can go to the connection corner with you to learn mindfulness skills. You can practice these strategies together in the form of games, activities, movement, and breathing. Practiced regularly, these skills can help your child enhance and maintain a sense of well-being. Your child can also use these skills when they're experiencing difficult emotions.

* **Supportive space:** The connection corner is a place for your child to go with you to work through a difficult emotion. When this happens, you can also work on your own calming strategies in order to be a soothing presence for your child. This is part of the coregulation process that we talked about in chapter 1. With time, your child may come to associate this space with feeling better. It could even become a place they'll want to go to calm themselves down.

Below are the *where, how,* and *when* of your connection corner.

Where

First, decide together where your connection corner will be located in your home. It doesn't need to be a large space, just big enough for the two of you to sit or lie down comfortably. It doesn't need to be a dedicated space either. You can keep your materials in a box, so you can easily set up at a table or a spot on the floor.

How

Your connection corner is a space you'll visit frequently, ideally each day, so make it cozy and inviting—a place you both look forward to spending time in. Talk with your child about what you want your connection corner to look like or make a drawing of it together.

Here are items you may want in your space:

* pillows
* blankets
* craft supplies (and a basket or box to keep them in)
    * paper
    * crayons, markers, or colored pencils
    * glue stick
    * scissors
* stuffed animals
* favorite books (including this one!)
* notebook or journal (optional)

Once your connection corner is complete, sit down in it together for a few moments and simply notice how you feel in the space.

Tip: Try to keep your connection corner as uncluttered as possible. You don't need much to make it special.

When

Figure out the best time of day to use your space. Think of a time when neither of you is too tired or hungry and you won't feel rushed. (Even though your practice may be only five minutes long, if you keep checking the time so you're not late to the next thing, you're not going to be present.) Chapter 9 will help you set up a daily mindfulness practice schedule.

Tip: As you think about the best time of day to practice with your child, consider barriers, such as schedule changes, cranky moods, and looming to-do lists, that may arise and how you might work around them.

No Expectations

By now, you may have an image in your mind of you and your child happily practicing mindfulness together each day. However, it's better for both of you if you go into it with no expectations of how it will actually play out.

If you're excited to create your connection corner but your child doesn't seem interested, give them some time. If they feel forced into it, it won't be a calming space for them. Consider the following to pique their interest:

✷ Begin creating the space on your own and make it irresistible (you can always make changes later with their input). A blanket fort with a secret password to gain entrance couldn't be more enticing!

✷ Spend time in the space when they're nearby without any nudging for them to join you. Let them see you snuggled in a blanket while reading this book, drawing, or practicing some breaths from chapter 3.

✷ Tailor a few of the activities in chapters 3 through 8 to specific interests of theirs. For example, ask them to help you create a breath themed around their favorite superhero or TV show (see page 44).

Reconnection Space

The connection corner is a space where you and your child can practice mindfulness, learn to better manage your emotions, and calm your nervous systems. It can also be used as a space to wait out a meltdown and then reconnect with your child.

Once a meltdown has started, there's typically not much you can do besides making sure your child is safe and keeping yourself calm. When it's over, you can take them to the connection corner for a reset:

✷ Help them calm their nervous system. Give them a big hug, then shake it out (see page 67).

✷ Validate their feelings. Let them know you get it. For example, you might say, "You were really upset when you heard the game was canceled."

* When your child is ready to talk about it, give them your full attention and simply listen.

* Gently introduce a calming strategy by doing one yourself, such as belly breathing (see page 36). Invite them to choose the next one.

* When your child is ready to talk, you can problem-solve together. Without judgment or shaming, talk through what they could do differently next time.

Introducing Mindfulness

It's not imperative for your child to have a firm understanding of mindfulness before you begin practicing together in your connection corner. Over time, they'll recognize that they feel more focused and less anxious after spending time there. Once they've made that connection, the concept of mindfulness will be less abstract for them, and you can discuss what it is and why it's beneficial for both of you.

When you're ready to introduce them to the concept of mindfulness, try this simple explanation:

Mindfulness means paying attention to what's happening around you: what you can see, hear, taste, touch, and smell. It's also about noticing what's happening inside you: how you're feeling and the thoughts you're thinking. When you know what's going on around you and inside of you, you can make a better choice about what to do next. When you practice mindfulness, you're learning different ways to feel calm, focused, and more connected to yourself and others.

Provide relatable examples of times you've been mindful—maybe while taking a walk in nature or using your breath to feel calmer—and ask your child to think of their own examples. Ask them what mindfulness means to them.

It's Practice Time

The next six chapters are filled with the activities, breaths, movements, and crafts you and your child can practice in the connection corner. Take some time to explore the activities together—read them aloud, talk about them, and then decide on a few you'd like to try first and bookmark them.

Tip: I recommend belly breathing on page 36 as your very first practice. After that, feel free to move through the other activities in any order you choose.

I highly encourage you to personalize your practice and have fun. At the end of each chapter is a prompt to discuss or write down the activities that you and your child tried and any ideas the two of you had. If there is a different way you'd like to do any of the activities, feel free to adjust them and note the changes in your journal or this book.

Chapter 3

BREATHE

Your breath is like a superpower: it can calm your body, which calms your brain, and you always have it with you. When your brain is calm, it's easier for you and your child to think, focus, and notice how you're feeling.

The activities in this chapter will help you and your child get to know your breath a little better. The two of you will learn lots of different, fun ways to breathe, which you can try together in the connection corner.

Some breaths you'll do while being still. Others will get you up and moving. You'll also have a chance to create your very own mindful breaths. Over time, exploring different breaths will help your child make the connection between their breathing and how they feel.

Belly Breathing

Many mindful activities rely on belly breathing, so it's an important skill to master. In fact, this might be the most important activity in this entire book!

1. Sit comfortably next to or facing each other.

2. Put your hands on your belly.

3. Take a slow, quiet breath in through your nose and feel your belly fill up like a balloon.

4. Breathe out through your nose or mouth slowly and quietly. Let all the air out.

5. Repeat as many times as you'd like. Notice how you feel.

Let's Pause

Ocean Waves

Like your breath, waves are always coming and going. Breathe like the ocean when you want to feel relaxed.

1. Sit comfortably next to or facing each other.

2. Take a slow breath in through your nose as you pay attention to the sound of breathing in. Imagine a wave rolling onto the shore.

3. Pause for a moment, then slowly breathe out of your nose as you pay attention to the sound of breathing out. Imagine the wave rolling back to the sea.

4. Pause for a moment and begin again.

5. Repeat as many times as you'd like.

Alligator Breathing

Now try coordinating some movement with your breathing. Help these alligators take some breaths.

1. Sit comfortably or stand next to or facing each other.

2. Begin with the biggest alligator: Extend your arms long with your palms together like a giant alligator mouth, then breathe in and open your arms wide. Breathe out and bring your hands back together.

3. Next is the medium-size alligator: Stack your hands with your palms together. Breathe in and open your hands. Breathe out and close your hands.

4. Now the tiniest alligator: Stack your index finger over your thumb. Breathe in and open your fingers. Breathe out and close your fingers.

5. After your tiniest alligator breath, tuck your tiny alligator in your pocket. You can take it out to breathe with you whenever you need it.

Mindful Breathing

Take a few mindful moments to slow down and get to know your breath better.

1. Sit facing each other and pay extra close attention to your own breath for a few moments.

2. Notice where you felt your breath the most. Was it your chest? Your nose? Your belly?

3. Now hold your hand in front of your own nose and breathe. Do you notice warm or cool air?

4. Breathe in and follow your breath's path as it travels up your nose, down your throat, and into your lungs and belly.

5. Breathe out and follow your breath's path as it goes from your belly and lungs, up your throat, and out of your nose.

6. Repeat as many times as you'd like. Talk about what you felt and noticed.

Let's Connect

Match Your Breath

In this activity, you and your child will sync your breathing. Matching your breath can leave both of you feeling calm and focused.

1. Sit facing each other and be as still as you can.

2. Begin taking belly breaths (see page 36) and see if you can match each other's breathing rhythm.

3. After a few moments of breathing together, turn around and sit back-to-back.

4. Begin your belly breathing again.

5. Notice the other person's back moving as they breathe. Try to match your breath to theirs again. Continue as long as you'd like.

Let's Move

Fireworks Breathing

Fireworks explode in colors that move across the sky after they pop. Now *you* can be the fireworks!

1 Crouch down and press your palms together by your heart.

2 As you breathe in, stand up and raise your pressed palms above your head like fireworks shooting into the sky.

3 Hold your breath as you clap your hands together one time to make the sound of the fireworks.

4 Breathe out and slowly wiggle your fingers as you move your hands back down, like sparkly, shimmering fireworks in the sky.

5 Repeat as many times as you'd like. What colors were both of your fireworks?

Let's Move

Bend and Breathe

Take your time as you match your breath to these movements. Notice how the slow stretches and deep breaths feel together.

1. Begin standing across from each other with your feet apart and your arms out to the side. Take a deep breath in.

2. Breathe out slowly as you bend to one side and gently stretch. Reach one arm down and one arm up.

3. Breathe in slowly and come back to center.

4. Breathe out slowly as you bend to the other side and gently stretch. Reach one arm down and one arm up.

5. Breathe in and come back to center.

6. Repeat as many times as you'd like.

Let's Move

Jellyfish Breathing

Imagine you're a jellyfish. Sometimes jellyfish wiggle through the water, and sometimes they just peacefully float along.

1 Lie side-by-side on your backs.

2 Lift your arms and legs straight up.

3 Breathe in and wiggle your arms and legs like a swimming jellyfish.

4 Breathe out as you stop wiggling and slowly rock side to side like you're floating.

5 Repeat as many times as you'd like.

Let's Create

Create Your Own Breaths

Try making up your own breaths, using belly breathing (see page 36) as the foundation. Whether you're standing and moving or sitting quietly, the only rule is to make sure you can easily breathe in and out.

Start by making up some animal breaths. Here are some to try:

* elephant
* sloth
* tiger
* swan
* unicorn

Here are some additional ideas:

* mountain
* elevator
* rain
* airplane
* flower
* superhero

Breath Cards

Create your own breath cards and decorate a box to keep them in.

Materials
* pen or pencil
* index cards or paper cut into card-size pieces
* crayons, markers, or colored pencils
* small cardboard box (like an empty tissue box or shoebox)

1. Sit together on the floor or at a table.

2. Draw or write down different breaths you learned or made up (see previous page) on the index cards. These are your breath cards.

3. Decorate your box any way you'd like using crayons, markers, or colored pencils.

4. Put the breath cards into the box.

5. Take turns choosing breath cards from the box (no peeking). Each time, practice the breath that's written on the card together.

6. As you learn and create more breaths, make more cards and add them to your box.

Let's Reflect

Discuss with your child the activities from this chapter that you tried, what you each noticed while practicing, things you might do differently, and any other ideas. If you're keeping a journal, add some notes.

Chapter 4

FOCUS

An increased ability to focus helps us become more self-aware and better able to respond thoughtfully. In this chapter, you and your child will use your senses to practice focusing on the present moment.

Mindfulness means paying attention to what's happening now, but sometimes paying attention can be tough. Lots of things distract us, including our own thoughts and feelings. Our senses (what we see, hear, smell, taste, and touch) and our breath are always there to help us get back on track.

The activities in this chapter will help you and your child feel more connected to yourselves, each other, and everything around you. From mindful listening (a great foundational mindfulness skill) and buzzing like a bumblebee to guessing games and hunting for treasure, see how mindfulness can pique your curiosity.

Mindful Listening

One of the simplest ways to practice mindfulness is to listen to the sounds around you. No matter where you are, you can always practice mindful listening.

1. Sit comfortably next to or across from each other and be as still as you can.

2. Listen closely to the sounds around you for a few moments.

3. Compare what you heard.
   - How many different sounds did you hear?
   - What was the loudest sound you heard? What was the softest?
   - What was the farthest sound you heard? What was the closest?

Tip: Try mindful listening with a chime or bell. Focus all your attention on that single sound until it fades and you can no longer hear it.

Let's Pause

Mindful Eating

When you and your child eat mindfully, you take your time and focus on using all of your senses. As you explore each sense, talk about your experiences.

1. Sit together at a table.

2. Pick up the food and notice how it feels in your hands.

3. Look at the colors and any markings on the food. Notice the shape.

4. Smell the food. Does smelling it make you want to take a bite?

5. Take a small bite to taste the food. Chew it and swallow it slowly. Notice how it feels on your tongue and as it moves down your throat.

6. Listen. Does your food make a sound when you bite into it?

7. Continue to eat your food slowly, paying attention to the experience.

8. Talk about your experience. How did your food taste? If you've eaten it before, did it taste better this time? Did you enjoy taking your time, or was your brain telling you to hurry up?

Tip: Good foods to use when you practice mindful eating are raisins, apples, or berries—but you can eat anything mindfully.

Bumblebee Breathing

Picture a bumblebee buzzing around a flower patch. Notice how this breath sounds and feels as you try to mimic it two different ways.

1. Sit comfortably next to or across from each other and be as still as you can.

2. Breathe in slowly through your nose and as you breathe out, make a humming sound—hmmmmmmmm.

3. Now cover your ears with your hands and try it again—hmmmmmmmm.

4. How was it different the second time?

5. Practice your bumblebee breath a few more times (with your ears covered or uncovered, your choice) and notice how you feel.

3-2-1 Focus

This activity is a quick way to get focused using three of your senses. As you play, keep your answers in your head, and then compare what you saw, heard, and felt at the end.

1. Sit comfortably next to or across from each other.

2. Decide who will lead first. The leader chooses a color.

3. Look around the room for three things in that color.

4. Then listen for two different sounds.

5. Finally, touch one thing that's near you and think of words that describe it.

6. Compare your answers. Switch leaders and choose a new color.

Guess the Shape

In this activity, you and your child take turns using your index fingers to draw shapes on each other's backs. The guessing is fun, and the drawing can feel soothing.

1. Decide who will draw first. Sit down with the person who is drawing first facing the other person's back.

2. As that person draws a shape on the other's back, the other person guesses what the shape is.

3. After a few shapes, switch places.

4. Feel free to change the category to letters, numbers, or simple drawings.

Tip: If drawing feels too tickly, try applying a bit more pressure.

Let's Move

Check Your Balance

Practice your balancing skills together. There's a challenge at the end!

1. Stand side by side with your hands on your hips.

2. Look straight ahead at something that's not moving. This is your focal point.

3. Lift your right foot a few inches off the ground. Keep your eyes on your focal point.

4. Breathe mindfully as you balance for a few moments. Put your foot down.

5. Repeat steps 2–4 with your left foot.

6. Did you balance better on your right or left side, or did they feel the same?

7. For fun, try balancing with your eyes closed. How did you do?

Let's Move

Mindful Mirror

Imagine you're looking into a mirror. Be mindful of what you see and try to copy your partner's moves as best you can.

1. Sit across from each other. Choose one person to be the leader and one to be the mirror.

2. The leader holds up their hands and moves them in different ways: making circles, moving up and down, or wiggling fingers.

3. The "mirror" tries to copy the movements exactly.

4. After a few moments, switch who's the leader and the mirror and play again.

5. Talk about how it felt to mimic each other's movements.

Tip: To make the game a bit more challenging, try the following:

✳ Stand up and move your whole body.

✳ Try some dance moves.

✳ Switch from going in slow motion to super fast.

Get Unstuck

Sometimes it's hard to pay attention and focus because you're stuck in the future (thinking about something that might happen) or you're stuck in the past (thinking about something that already happened). Focusing on your senses can help you get unstuck. You and your child can try a few of these mindfulness strategies to quickly shift your thoughts to the present moment:

Look around and name things you see.

From where you're sitting or standing, list the different colors you see.

Put all your attention on your feet. Place them firmly on the ground. Are they cold, hot, or just right? How does it feel to wiggle your toes?

Place your hand on your heart and notice how that feels.

Listen for the farthest sound and the closest sound.

Let's Create

Memory Drawing

Try to remember and draw as many details as you can about a space that you're in every day.

Materials
* paper
* crayons, markers, or colored pencils

1. Sit together on the floor or at a table.

2. Close your eyes for a moment and think about a room in your home (not the one you're in now).

3. Try your best to draw the room from memory. Add in as many details as you can remember.

4. When you're finished, go to the room and compare your drawing to what you see now. Did you miss anything?

5. Show each other your drawings and compare what you drew.

Let's Create

Treasure Hunt

If you've ever wanted to find buried treasure, now's your chance! For this activity, you'll each create a treasure and a map for the other person.

Materials
* whatever you need to create your treasure
* paper
* crayons, markers, or colored pencils

1. Sit on the floor or at a table but far enough away from each other that you can't see each other working.

2. Make a "treasure" for the other person. This can be a special drawing, a note, or any small homemade gift.

3. Next, take turns hiding your treasure somewhere in your home.

4. Create a map that starts in the connection corner and leads to the treasure.

5. Give the other person the map you made and wish them luck as they go on their treasure hunt.

6. Once you each discover your treasure, talk about how it felt when you found your treasure, and how you felt while making and hiding the other person's treasure.

Let's Reflect

Discuss with your child the activities from this chapter that you tried, what you each noticed while practicing, things you might do differently, and any other ideas. If you're keeping a journal, add some notes.

Chapter 5

Being able to notice and name your feelings is an important mindfulness skill. As you practice building this skill together and your child's emotional self-awareness grows, they'll also become more attuned to others' feelings, which increases their sense of empathy and compassion. You'll also learn ways to work through more challenging emotions.

Think of feelings as visitors. Some come and go quietly, and others are big and loud and want to stick around. If you ignore them, they usually get even louder. A great strategy for handling big emotions is to notice them and name them. They'll begin to quiet down, giving you the chance to decide what to do next.

In this chapter, you and your child will make your own feelings card deck and bracelets to help you explore what your emotions look and feel like. Then, from quietly counting clouds to shaking it out from head to toe, you'll learn different ways to handle feelings that visit you.

Let's pause

Five-Count Breathe Out

Mindful breathing is soothing for your brain and body. A long, slow exhale is especially helpful when you're feeling angry or frustrated.

1. Sit comfortably next to or across from each other.

2. Breathe in while slowly counting to three in your head. Hold up your fingers for a counting visual. Try to follow your child's pace.

3. Breathe out while slowly counting to five in your head. Hold up your fingers for a counting visual. Try to follow your child's pace.

4. Continue for a few more breaths, then talk about how you feel.

Name It to Tame It

Psychiatrist Dan Siegel (see Resources) said that if you identify the emotion you are feeling ("name it") then you can prevent it from taking over ("tame it"). When you're experiencing an overwhelming feeling, simply naming it can cause a reaction in your brain that begins to calm your nervous system.

Labeling your feelings in front of your child models this strategy. Plus it lets your child know that you also experience difficult feelings from time to time. Regularly invite your child to name their feelings. You can practice naming feelings together by doing the activities on pages 62, 68, and 71.

Let's Connect

Feelings Faces

Get to know your feelings a bit better by noticing what you look like when different feelings are visiting.

Materials
✴ mirror

1 Sit together in front of a mirror.

2 Take turns naming feelings. When one of you names a feeling, both of you show what you think your face would look like if you had that feeling.

3 Say the feeling out loud as you show it. For example, say "I feel angry!" or "I feel happy!"

4 Notice your body language for each feeling. What do your shoulders, arms, hands, and legs look like when you're showing each feeling?

5 Talk about how each feeling looked and felt.

6 Optional: After this activity, draw faces that represent different feelings (see page 71).

Tip: Remind your child that all feelings—even the ones that don't feel good—are okay to have.

Let's Connect

Share a Song

Songs can sometimes bring up feelings. In this activity, you and your child will share songs with each other and notice the feelings that show up.

Materials
✳ device that plays music

1 Sit comfortably next to or across from each other.

2 Think of songs that make you feel happy when you listen to them.

3 Choose which one of you will pick a song first.

4 Play the first person's song. Listen to the song together and pay attention to how you feel.

5 Talk about how you felt and why. Was it the words in the song? Was it the music? Did the song remind you of something?

6 Repeat steps 4 and 5 with the other person's song.

Tip: If a song makes you feel like dancing, have a dance party!

Our Mindful Brains

Children can feel empowered when they understand the science behind why they react the way they do to big feelings. Once you've tried some of the activities in this chapter, consider sharing this explanation of the science of mindfulness:

There's a part of your brain—we'll call it your animal brain—whose job is to protect you from big feelings. (Grown-ups have an animal brain, too!) When you're angry, frustrated, scared, or worried, your animal brain tells you to fight, run away, or stay very still. Think of a time you were scared and wanted to run and hide. That was your animal brain trying to keep you safe.

When your animal brain is in control, your thinking brain takes a break, and it's much harder to make choices or solve problems. The cool part is that you have the power to get your thinking brain working again! And it's so simple: just pause and take a few slow breaths. Pausing and taking some slow breaths is being mindful. Being mindful gets your thinking brain working again, so you can figure out what to do next or ask someone for help. You may still feel the big feeling, but now you—and not your animal brain—can decide what to do with it.

Let's Move

Sigh It Out Loud

It can feel good to let out a loud sigh. When you're feeling stressed or need a quick break, just let it out.

1. Stand next to or across from each other.

2. Breathe in and scrunch your shoulders toward your ears.

3. As you breathe out, relax your shoulders and let out a big sigh: *Huh!*

4. Breathe in and lift up your heels.

5. As you breathe out, drop your heels and let out another sigh: *Huh!*

6. Now put the movements together. Breathe in and scrunch your shoulders as you lift your heels.

7. Breathe out as you drop your shoulders and your heels and sigh: *Huh!*

Volcano Jumps

Sometimes you might feel like a volcano that's ready to erupt. Try this activity when you're feeling frustrated or if you just have a lot of energy.

1. Crouch down with lots of room between the two of you.

2. Scrunch your face and shoulders, make fists, and begin to shake. Imagine you're getting hotter and ready to explode.

3. Jump up high as you reach your hands in the air.

4. Land standing on your feet and notice how that felt.

5. Try a few more volcano jumps if you'd like.

Let's Move

Shake It Out

Shaking it out is a great way to relieve stress, boost energy, and reset. Notice how your body feels before and after you shake it out.

1. Stand up and make sure you have room to move.

2. Put one hand on your heart and see if you can notice it beating. Put your hand down.

3. Put your other hand on your belly. Notice how fast you're breathing. Put your hand down.

4. Shake your whole body from head to toe as fast as you can.

5. After a few moments, pause. Put one hand on your heart and the other on your belly.

6. Check in with your heartbeat and your breath again. Has anything changed?

7. Take five belly breaths (see page 36) and notice how you feel now.

Tip: Try this exercise when a big feeling visits and you'd like to feel calmer.

Feelings Bracelets

Feelings bracelets let you pause and name how you're feeling. This can help you take the time to savor good feelings. When you have a more challenging feeling, simply noticing and naming it can make it feel a little smaller.

Materials
✸ different-colored plastic beads
✸ string or elastic, two bracelet-size strands

1. Sit together at a table or on the floor.

2. Sort the beads by color.

3. Talk about some of your most common feelings. Make a list of feelings the same number as bead colors.

4. Assign each feeling a color. For example, red might mean angry, yellow might mean frustrated, and blue might mean happy.

5. String beads of all the different colors on the string or elastic strands, tie the ends, and put on your bracelets.

How to use your feelings bracelets
✸ Take turns touching a bead and name the feeling the color represents. Then tell about a time you felt that way.
✸ Any time one of these feelings visits you, touch the bead color that matches the feeling. Next, label the feeling in your head by saying to yourself, *I feel [name the emotion]*. Then take a deep breath.

Let's Create

Counting Clouds

Bring your mind into the present moment while slowly counting clouds.

Materials

✳ 10 cotton balls for younger children or up to 20 for older children
✳ small bag or box to store the cotton balls
✳ googly eyes and glue (optional)

1 Put the cotton balls in the bag or box.

2 Sit comfortably with your bag or box of cotton balls in front of you. Imagine it's filled with clouds and the floor is the sky.

3 Have your child take their time pulling out one cloud at a time and placing it on the floor. Count them together as you go.

4 Optionally, after counting, take turns picking up a cloud and telling it something that's worrying you. Imagine the cloud (and your worry) floating away as you put it back in the bag or box. Repeat as many times as you and your child would like.

Tip: For bigger clouds with a bit more personality, glue three cotton balls together and then glue on some googly eyes.

Let's Create

How I Feel Better

Make your own posters showing things you do that help you feel better when a difficult feeling visits you.

Materials
* crayons, markers, or colored pencils
* paper

1. Sit together on the floor or at a table.

2. Talk about what each of you does to feel better when a difficult feeling visits.

3. Draw things that make you feel better on a piece of paper. (Grab more paper if you need it.)

4. Post your drawing in the connection corner or put it in your joy book (see page 82).

5. Next time a difficult feeling visits, say how you feel and do an activity from the ones you drew.

Here are some things that might help you feel better:
* talk to someone
* take a break in a quiet place
* read
* drink some water
* hug a person, pet, pillow, or stuffed animal
* take deep breaths
* listen to music
* move your body (run, dance, play)
* draw
* daydream
* count to ten or higher
* color

Let's Create

Feelings Face Cards

Create your own feelings face cards.

Materials
* crayons, markers, or colored pencils
* index cards or paper cut into card-size pieces

1. Sit together on the floor or at a table.
2. Practice making feelings faces together in a mirror (see page 62).
3. Choose a few feelings you'd like to draw.
4. Draw a face on each card that represents one of the feelings. It can be a person's or a made-up creature's face.
5. Choose an activity below.

How to use your feelings face cards
* Place your cards upside down and take turns choosing a card. Turn it over, make the face that's on the card, and tell about a time you felt that way.
* Choose a card and make up a story about why the person or creature on the card feels that way.
* Play feelings charades: choose a card (don't let the other person see it) and act out the feeling while the other person guesses what it is.
* When you check in (see page 101), choose the card that shows how you're feeling at that moment.

Let's Reflect

Discuss with your child the activities from this chapter that you tried, what you each noticed while practicing, things you might do differently, and any other ideas. If you're keeping a journal, add some notes.

Chapter 6

CARE

Think about what makes you smile, what fills up your heart, and what makes you want to celebrate. That's your joy! This chapter focuses on you and your child finding, appreciating, and sharing joy and kindness in everyday life.

When you pay attention to the people and things that bring you joy—and especially when you practice gratitude for them—a cool thing happens: you begin to notice more joy all around you, and you want to share it with others. Kindness is another caring way to cultivate joy—in others as well as yourself. Sharing kindness helps us feel more connected to each other and builds empathy and compassion.

In this chapter, you and your child will explore new ways to express gratitude and kindness. You'll also celebrate the small things, notice the good stuff, and create a joy book.

Let's Pause

Fill Up Your Heart

When you think about the things you love, it can feel like your heart is filling up with joy! Take a few moments to savor this feeling.

1. Sit comfortably next to or across from each other. Place your hands on your heart.

2. Close your eyes, if you'd like. Be as still as you can.

3. Think about people, animals, things, and places you love.

4. Each time you think of something you love, breathe in and out slowly and focus on the feeling in your heart.

5. After you're done, talk about what you each thought about and how it made you feel.

Let's Pause

Three Wishes

Send three wishes to someone you care about.

1. Sit comfortably next to or across from each other.
2. Close your eyes, if you'd like, and think of someone you care about.
3. Breathe in and think of a wish for that person.
4. Gently blow as you breathe out, like you're blowing the wish into the sky.
5. Repeat this two more times, for a total of three wishes.
6. Talk about how it felt to send those wishes.

Tip: You don't have to get fancy with your wishes—you can simply wish your person happiness, peace, and love.

Let's Connect

Kindness Notes

In this activity, you'll create special notes for each other to find. Notice how it feels to both give and receive kindness.

Materials
✳ pencil, crayons, markers, or colored pencils
✳ paper

1 Sit so you're not facing each other.

2 Write the other person a short note on a piece of paper, telling them something you love about them. You could also draw them a picture.

3 Take turns looking away while the other person hides the note someplace for you to find later.

4 Think about how the other person will feel when they find your note.

5 Later, when you find the note meant for you, pause and notice how it feels when you read it.

6 Talk about how it feels to do something kind and how it feels when others are kind to you.

Tip: Make kindness notes for anyone else who lives in your home and hide them, too.

Let's Connect

Celebrate the Small Stuff

We often celebrate the big events in life, like birthdays and holidays. In this activity, you'll plan a celebration for a small special moment.

1. Sit comfortably next to or across from each other.

2. Talk about ways your family celebrates special occasions.

3. Next, talk about small, special moments that make you smile, like exploring a new park or having a grandparent visit. Choose one moment you'd like to celebrate next time it happens.

4. Plan a celebration for that moment. Would you decorate? Make up a silly dance? Give a speech? Make a card?

5. Next time that small moment happens, take some time to celebrate it.

Hug It Out

Hugs are a simple way to connect. Long, snuggly hugs reduce stress and simply feel great.

1 Stand facing each other.

2 Hug each other close while taking several deep breaths.

3 Afterward, talk about how the hug made you feel.

Tip: See if you can match your breathing as you hug.

Let's Move

Sprinkle Kindness

Think about what it would be like if the world were covered with kindness. In this activity, you and your child pretend you have the power to sprinkle kindness everywhere.

1. Stand up tall, making sure you both have space to move.

2. Tell each other about places where you'd like to sprinkle some kindness.

3. Bend your knees, reach down, and imagine gathering up as much kindness as you can.

4. Lift it above your head and wave your hands all around as you sprinkle the kindness to those places.

5. Choose a few more places that could use some kindness and keep going.

6. Talk about how it feels to sprinkle all that kindness around.

Tip: Add some breath to the movement: breathe in while you gather up your kindness and breathe out when you sprinkle it.

Let's Move

Catch the Good

Gratitude means focusing on the good things in your life and being thankful for all that you have. Roll the ball back and forth as you practice gratitude.

Materials
✳ ball

1 Sit across from each other. One of you starts with the ball.

2 Pause and think about things you're grateful for.

3 Say together, "We are grateful for . . . "

4 Whoever has the ball says one thing they're grateful for and rolls the ball to the other person.

5 As soon as the other person catches the ball, they say one thing they're grateful for and roll it back. Say whatever pops into your head and try to keep the ball moving.

6 Pause at some point to notice how you both feel.

Let's Create

Kindness Rocks!

Leave special messages around your community for people to find.

Materials

✹ markers (Sharpies work well) or paint and paintbrushes

✹ stones large enough to write words on (preferably light colored)

1. Sit together on the floor or at a table.

2. Write or paint a kind message on each stone, like "You are loved" or "You are amazing."

3. Decorate the rest of the stone any way you'd like.

4. Make as many stones as you'd like.

5. Place the stones around your community for others to find. Leave them in places where people will easily find them (but not trip over them).

6. Talk about how people might feel when they find a stone.

Let's Create

Joy Book

A joy book is a place to collect printed things, like drawings or words, that bring you joy when you look at or read them. You and your child can each make your own joy book, or you can make one together. The idea is to fill up your joy book over time with drawings, writing, photos, poems, words, or pictures cut from magazines—whatever makes you smile.

Materials

* ✳ three-ring binder (a blank notebook will also work)
* ✳ prepunched binder paper, or paper that fits in the binder and a hole punch
* ✳ crayons, markers, or colored pencils

1 Sit together on the floor or at a table. Talk for a few moments about what brings you joy.

2 Make a cover for your joy book on a piece of paper that will fit in the binder's cover sleeve. Decorate it any way you'd like. (If you're using a notebook, decorate the cover.)

3 Put paper in the binder.

4 On the first page, draw or list things that bring you joy from one of the following categories:
  * people
  * memories
  * animals
  * places

How to use your joy book

✳ Add to your joy book over time.

✳ Look through your joy book whenever you need a little joy.

Tip: Keep your joy book in a prominent place in your connection corner.

Let's Reflect

Discuss with your child the activities from this chapter that you tried, what you each noticed while practicing, things you might do differently, and any other ideas. If you're keeping a journal, add some notes.

Chapter 7

REST

While simply being in the connection corner offers a break from the busyness of the day, the activities in this chapter are designed to create a sense of deeper relaxation. By doing them with your child, you're modeling the importance of taking time to slow down and rest.

You'll learn to relax your bodies with a progressive muscle relaxation, some calming movements, and a chance to be still with a dragonfly. You'll also calm your minds with images of rainbows, starfish, and the most peaceful place you can imagine.

Bonus: Because the activities in this chapter are designed to help you and your child relax, they're perfect to do right before bedtime!

Let's Pause

Squeeze and Release

Stress can leave your muscles feeling tense and tight. This activity helps you relax from head to toes. If your child understands the pattern, you can each do this in silence. Alternatively, you can talk your child through each part of the body as you focus on it.

1. Sit comfortably next to or across from each other, or lie down on your backs.

2. Notice if anywhere in your body feels tense.

3. Breathe in and squeeze all the muscles in your face. Hold for three seconds, then breathe out and relax those muscles.

4. Repeat that same pattern—breathe in, squeeze, hold for three seconds, breathe out, and release—as you move through the following parts of your body:
   - shoulders
   - arms
   - hands
   - belly
   - legs
   - feet

5. Talk about what you noticed and how you feel now.

My Mindful Friend

This simple breath can be calming for both of you—and a couple of favorite stuffed animals. Get comfy and watch them go for a ride.

Materials
* two pillows
* two small stuffed animals

1. Lie down on your backs next to each other with pillows under your heads. Each of you do the following steps.

2. Place one of the stuffed animals on your belly.

3. Breathe in and watch the stuffed animal go up.

4. Breathe out and watch the stuffed animal go back down.

5. Take a few more slow breaths and give the stuffed animal a relaxing ride.

6. End by giving the stuffed animal a big hug.

Let's Pause

Relaxing Rainbow

Be mindful of what you see and let the colors of the rainbow help you feel relaxed and calm.

1. Sit comfortably next to or across from each other.

2. Say out loud a color of the rainbow, starting with red.

3. Take a few moments to look at all the red things you see around you. (Keep your answers in your head for now.)

4. Continue by naming the remaining rainbow colors: orange, yellow, green, blue, and purple. Pause between each color while you look around.

5. Talk about how you feel and the different things you saw.

Tip: Consider drawing a rainbow in your joy book (see page 82).

Let's Connect

Starfish Breathing

Starfish breathing is relaxing and can also feel very soothing. Take your time with this breath.

1. Sit across from one another. One of you is the tracer; the other is the starfish.

2. The starfish holds out their hand, palm side up and fingers spread wide.

3. The tracer places their index finger in the center of the starfish's palm.

4. Both of you breathe in slowly as the tracer moves their finger from the center of the starfish's palm to the tip of the pinky finger.

5. Both of you breathe out slowly as the tracer's finger follows the same line back to the center of the palm.

6. Continue this pattern with each finger. Breathe in when the tracer moves their finger up one of the starfish's fingers. Breathe out when the tracer follows the same line back down to the center of the palm.

7. Switch who's the tracer and the starfish and try it again.

Tip: If the tracing feels too tickly, try applying a bit more pressure.

Let's Connect

Gift Box Meditation

You'll both need your imaginations for this activity. Although you're the narrator, both of you get a gift box to open.

1 Have your child sit or lie down comfortably and close their eyes, if they'd like.

2 Slowly read the following:
Imagine that you are walking through a grassy meadow. It's a beautiful, warm day. You see flowers and trees, and you hear birds singing. You walk toward one of the trees. You see something near the trunk of the tree, and you're curious about it. As you get closer, you see that it's a box with a ribbon tied around it. It's a present. It has a gift tag attached to it. You sit down next to it and look closer. The name on the gift tag is your name. You pull off the ribbon and open the box. What do you see inside?

3 Both of you spend a few moments imagining what would be in your gift box. There are no rules—let your imaginations go!

4 Open your eyes and sit up if you were lying down.

5 Talk about how you both felt as you walked through the meadow, when you saw the box, and when you saw your name on the gift tag. Then talk about what was in your gift boxes.

Legs Up the Wall

This pose, often done in yoga classes, is known as an inversion because your head is lower than your legs. Inversions relax your body and calm your mind.

1. Lie on your backs with hips on the floor and legs straight (or knees slightly bent) up against a wall.

2. Arms can rest next to you on the floor. Hold hands if you'd like.

3. Take slow belly breaths (see page 36).

4. When you're ready to stop, bend your knees and roll to one side, then sit up slowly.

Tip: You can also place a chair in front of you and rest your legs—with knees bent—on the chair.

Let's Move

Winding Down

When you're both ready to relax, wind yourselves down with these yoga-inspired moves.

1. Stand side by side and reach your arms straight up toward the ceiling.

2. Bend your knees slightly as you fold forward, letting your arms hang down. Take a breath.

3. Place your palms flat on the floor and walk your feet a few steps back. Take two breaths.

4. Gently lower your knees to the floor. Put the tops of your feet on the floor and sit back on your heels.

5. Walk your hands forward and then gently rest your forehead on the floor. If your head doesn't reach the floor, put a pillow or a folded blanket under it.

6. Take three breaths. Notice how you feel.

Tip: You can do this wind-down on bath or beach towels or yoga mats, if you'd like.

My Peaceful Place

Think about all the things that help you feel calm and relaxed, then use your imagination and dream up the most peaceful space.

Materials
- ✺ crayons, markers, or colored pencils
- ✺ paper
- ✺ timer

1 Sit together on the floor or at a table.

2 Take turns telling each other what you imagine your most peaceful place would be like. Get as detailed as possible. For example, describe colors, smells, textures, and sounds.

3 Draw your peaceful places with lots of details.

4 Lie down next to each other and set your timer for five minutes. Imagine yourself relaxing in your peaceful place until the timer goes off.

5 Talk about how it felt to spend time in your peaceful places.

Tip: Add your drawings to your joy book (see page 82).

Mindful Dragonfly

Dragonflies are busy insects. Even though they love to fly around, they also need to rest. In this activity, you'll create your own dragonflies, then help them pause their busy day and rest with you. (Parent note: If your child is not familiar with dragonflies, do a little research together before beginning this activity.)

Materials

- ✳ pencil
- ✳ paper
- ✳ dragonfly template (see page 120)
- ✳ crayons, markers, or colored pencils
- ✳ scissors
- ✳ glue
- ✳ two Popsicle sticks (or more, depending on how many dragonflies you'd like to make)
- ✳ googly eyes (optional)

How to make your dragonfly

1. Sit together on the floor or at a table.
2. Outline dragonfly wings on paper like the ones shown on page 120.
3. Color in the wings.
4. Cut the wings out and glue them to a Popsicle stick.
5. Draw two eyes on the top of the Popsicle stick, or glue on googly eyes.
6. Let the glue dry before using your dragonfly.

How to use your dragonfly

1. Sit comfortably next to or across from each other or lie down.

2. Choose a spot on your body where your dragonfly will rest (like the top of your head, shoulder, hand, or leg). Place your dragonfly on that spot.

3. Be as still as you can and take slow belly breaths (see page 36).

4. Let your dragonfly rest with you for as long as you'd like.

Tip: Make a few dragonflies and help them rest on a few different spots.

Let's Reflect

Discuss with your child the activities from this chapter that you tried, what you each noticed while practicing, things you might do differently, and any other ideas. If you're keeping a journal, add some notes.

Chapter 8

GO

Mindfulness can be practiced anytime and anywhere—it doesn't end when you leave the connection corner. Once you begin to regularly practice mindfulness, you'll see how it can naturally become a part of each day, no matter the location.

From a sunrise breath to an evening reflection, this chapter offers ways for you and your child to integrate your practice into things you do every day, whether at home or on the go.

To help you remember to sprinkle moments of mindfulness throughout the day, place reminder cards around your home. You'll soon find that any moment can be a mindful moment.

Sunrise Breathing

Sunrise breathing offers a mindful way to start your day. Consider making it a regular part of your morning routine, for example, by doing it together right after your child gets dressed.

1. Stand across from each other, arms at your sides.

2. Make a round (sun) shape with your arms in front of you and fingers touching.

3. Breathe in as you slowly reach your arms in a circle overhead. Imagine the sun rising.

4. Breathe out and slowly release your arms out to the side. Imagine sunlight spreading across the sky.

5. Complete two more sunrise breaths. Imagine the warmth of the sun on your face.

I Can Do It

This activity can help boost your child's confidence before they do something that feels difficult. Tapping along with the words can help them feel calm and ready.

1. Sit across from each other.

2. Choose four words that will give you confidence, like "I can do it" or "I am so strong."

3. Rest your hands on your lap, palms facing up.

4. Tap your pointer fingers to your thumbs as you say the first word out loud.

5. Tap your middle fingers to your thumbs as you say the second word out loud.

6. Tap your ring fingers to your thumbs as you say the third word out loud.

7. Tap your pinkie fingers to your thumbs as you say the fourth word out loud.

8. Repeat the pattern of tapping each finger and saying the words out loud a couple more times.

9. If your child would like, they can repeat the tapping pattern as they say the words in their head for a few moments.

Tip: You can do this activity together in the car, for example, when your child is about to try something new, like a sport.

Let's Pause

Make It Mindful

Think about some daily tasks you and your child do and how you can make them mindful by focusing on the senses. Let's use brushing your teeth as an example. Feel free to talk your child through the activity, especially when you're first learning it.

1. As you put the toothpaste on your toothbrush, notice the smell and color.

2. When you begin brushing, notice the taste of the toothpaste.

3. Notice the smell of the toothpaste.

4. Notice the feeling of the brush on your teeth and tongue.

5. Notice the movement of your hand and arm as you brush.

6. Notice the feeling of rinsing your mouth when you're done brushing.

7. After you put your toothbrush away, take a mindful breath: Make an "O" shape with your lips. Breathe in and out through your mouth and notice how it feels.

8. Talk about any differences you noticed between regular teeth brushing and mindful teeth brushing.

Tip: Talk about other daily tasks that you can do mindfully.

Check In

Encourage your child and remind yourself to pause and check in with yourselves throughout the day. Paying attention to how you feel physically and emotionally can help you slow down, take a moment, and make better choices. Feel free to prompt your child out loud, especially when you're first learning how to do this.

1 If you're at home, sit comfortably next to or across from each other. If you're out and about, simply pause and be still for a moment. You can do this in the car, outside, or while waiting in line, for example.

2 Notice what's happening in your body. Ask yourself questions like, *Am I warm or cold? Does my body feel slow or full of energy?*

3 Notice which feeling is visiting you right now. Is there more than one?

4 Finish your check-in with three belly breaths (see page 36).

5 Talk about what you each noticed during your check-in.

Tip: Checking in is a great way to begin and/or end your time in the connection corner.

Everyday Mindful Moments

You and your child can use different times during the day as reminders to check in with yourselves. Here are some examples:

when you wash your hands

before or after you eat

when you wake up or before you go to sleep

while waiting in a line

while you're filling up your water bottle

What else can you add to the list?

Evening Connection

In the evening, maybe right before bed, spend a few moments reflecting together on all the good things from your day. Even on the toughest of days, there's always something to be grateful for.

1 Sit comfortably or lie down next to each other.

2 Take a few belly breaths (see page 36) as you both think about your day.

3 Talk about the following:
  - something that made you smile and why
  - something kind you did for someone, or something kind that someone did for you
  - what you're looking forward to tomorrow

4 Notice how you feel.

Tip: If you'd like, draw or write about the good things from your day and add the drawing or note to your joy book (see page 82).

Mindful Storytime

There are so many different things to notice in a good children's book. Whether you choose a new book or an old favorite, slow down and read it together mindfully.

1 Choose a picture book you'd like to read together.

2 Sit comfortably next to each other. One of you will be the reader.

3 Take your time with the book. Notice the pictures, the characters, and any feelings that you have while you read or listen.

4 After you read or listen to the story, talk about the following:
- any feelings you noticed in yourself
- how the characters in the book felt
- what you liked about the pictures
- how the colors in the book made you feel
- how you felt about the story and why

Let's Move

Sensory Walk

Pay attention to your senses during a mindful walk. You can walk outside or indoors.

1. Go for a walk together. Take turns calling out the different senses.

2. One of you says "listen." Talk about whatever you hear, such as the sound of your footsteps on the ground.

3. Next, one of you says "look." Talk about what you see, including the biggest and the smallest things, the colors, and the farthest thing you can see.

4. Next, one of you says "smell." Talk about all the different smells, if they're pleasant, unpleasant, or neutral, and where they're coming from.

5. Then, one of you says "feel." Talk about how your breath feels, parts of you that are warm or cool, and any feelings that are visiting you.

6. Continue the walk and notice new things as the scenery changes.

Let's Move

Check-in Walk

Whether it's a walk to school or a longer weekend stroll, walks with your child can be a great time to check in with how both of you are feeling.

1. Before you set off, do a check-in (see page 101) and invite your child to do the same.

2. Talk about how you feel. For example, is your child excited or nervous before walking to school? Are you relaxed because it's the weekend?

3. While you're walking, point out anything that makes either of you smile.

4. Do another check-in at the end of the walk.

5. Talk about whether you feel the same now as when you started your walk.

6. Finish with a nice, long hug.

Let's Create

Our Mindful Days

Visual reminders are a great way to build new routines. Create a poster for your connection corner showing different ways you've practiced mindfulness together or on your own. Your poster will remind you to be mindful throughout the day.

Materials

- crayons, markers, or colored pencils
- index cards or paper cut into card-size pieces
- glue stick or thumbtacks
- large piece of cardstock or poster board, or a bulletin board

1. Sit together on the floor or at a table. Decide where your poster will be placed.

2. Talk about different ways you both have practiced mindfulness.

3. Draw on index cards what you did. If your child reads, you can also write the name of activities.

4. Glue your cards to the poster or tack them to the bulletin board.

5. Keep adding to your poster as you practice new mindfulness activities.

Mindful Reminders: Take Five

It's easy to practice mindfulness—the hard part is remembering to do it throughout the day. In this activity, you'll create reminders to place around your home.

Materials

- ✺ five pieces of paper, any size
- ✺ crayons, markers, or colored pencils
- ✺ tape (optional)

1 Sit together on the floor or at a table.

2 Decide how big your mindfulness reminders will be and what they will look like.

3 Decorate your reminders. Add words, if you'd like. They can be as simple or as detailed as you'd like. For example, one might simply say "breathe."

4 Place the reminder cards around your home together. Take five belly breaths (see page 36) each time you place one.

5 Whenever you walk by one of them, pause and take five belly breaths.

Tip: Move your reminder cards to different locations around your home from time to time so you'll continue to notice them.

Here are some other ways you can pause and "take five" when you come across one of your mindful reminders:

* ✴ Listen for five different sounds.
* ✴ Name five things you see.
* ✴ Find five things of a specific color.
* ✴ Think of five things you're grateful for.
* ✴ Find five things shaped like a square (or any shape you choose).
* ✴ Touch five things near you and notice how they feel.
* ✴ Repeat this sentence in your head five times: "I can take a pause."
* ✴ Look around and find five things that make you smile.
* ✴ Create your own "take five"!

Let's Reflect

Discuss with your child the activities from this chapter that you tried, what you each noticed while practicing, things you might do differently, and any other ideas. If you're keeping a journal, add some notes.

Chapter 9

PRACTICE

Congratulations! By this point, you and your child have set up your space, chosen a time to practice, and explored the mindful activities chapters. Let's pull it all together.

In this final chapter, we'll cover how to:

* make your practice a consistent habit (ideally daily)
* establish opening and closing routines
* create sample practice plans
* be mindful throughout the day

Note: Although this book is set up to help you and your child create a daily mindfulness practice, any amount of time that the two of you spend practicing together is beneficial. Some weeks or times of the year may be more hectic than others, so don't worry if your practice schedule becomes a bit inconsistent or even nonexistent. You can always begin again!

Aim for Consistency

Like exercise or playing an instrument, mindfulness has its greatest effect with consistent practice. After practicing consistently for a while, you'll likely find that mindfulness becomes part of how you live each day. You and your child may find yourselves more present, more aware of yourselves and everything around you, and more intentional about how you live.

Since new habits can be tough to establish, let's explore some ways to help you get into the routine of a daily practice:

✳ **Add mindfulness time to your daily schedule.** It sounds kind of obvious, but if you see it in writing among the other important tasks of your day, you're more likely to remember to do it.

✳ **Link your practice with another daily habit.** Think of something that you already do each day, for example, when your child comes home from school, and consider adding in your connection corner time either right before or right after that already established routine, chore, or task.

✳ **Set an alarm.** After you've chosen a time of day for your practice, set up a reminder on your phone. Name the alarm something that will make you smile like "time to relax" or "connection time with [your child's name]."

✳ **Make a practice plan.** If you map out exactly what you'd like to do for your next practice, it will be front of mind. There's a template on page 121 to help you plan a session. (See the sample plans in this chapter.) Of course, it's completely fine to change your plan once you start.

✳ **Create visual reminders.** See page 108 for the mindful reminders activity. These are perfect little nudges for both of you.

Establish Opening and Closing Routines

Structure, routine, and predictability are comforting—for children as well as adults. Consider establishing opening and closing routines, or brief practices that begin and end your time in the connection corner.

Transitioning to or from a current activity to a completely different activity can be tough for some kids. If you begin your time in the connection corner with a short, familiar routine, you and your child are better equipped to switch your brains into a different mode and ease into the space. A closing routine is also a helpful transition tool that signals to your brain that it's time to move on to something else.

Keep your opening and closing routines simple. For example, choose one or two from each list:

Opening routine ideas

- ✳ Belly Breathing (page 36)
- ✳ Mindful Listening (page 48)
- ✳ 3-2-1 Focus (page 51)
- ✳ Shake It Out (page 67)
- ✳ Check In (page 101)

Closing routine ideas

- ✳ Breath Cards (page 45)
- ✳ Fill Up Your Heart (page 74)
- ✳ Three Wishes (page 75)
- ✳ Hug It Out (page 78)
- ✳ Check In (page 101)

Putting It All Together

Once you've settled on your opening and closing routines, choose a few activities for your practice from chapters 3 to 8. Here are a few different ways to choose your activities:

- ✳ **Work your way through the chapters in order.** This way, you'll be sure to try each activity at least once. Keep a list of the activities you want to do again. You can also put stars next to your favorites.

- ✳ **Choose randomly.** Write down the activities you'd like to try on scraps of paper and put them in a basket (or any container). After your opening routine, take turns choosing activities from the basket.

- ✳ **Check in and choose.** Open your practice with a check-in (see page 101) to help determine the type of activity, or category, that feels right. For example, if you'd like an energy boost, opt for a Let's Move activity.

Make a Practice Plan

To help you establish a mindfulness practice, try making a practice plan. How much you do and how long you do it are up to you.

Some days, you and your child may have time for several activities and a craft. Other days, you may have only a few minutes to practice and may be tempted to skip it altogether. On those days, choose one activity or do your opening and/or closing routines only. It will take less than five minutes—you'll continue your momentum and still get a great practice in.

Here's an example of a practice plan:

Our Practice Plan

Date March 6   **Practice Time** 4:30 p.m.

Opening Routine
Mindful Listening for 1 minute (p. 48)

Our Practice
Mindful Eating (p. 49)
Mindful Dragonfly (p. 94)

Closing Routine
Choose a breath card and take 3 breaths (p. 45)
Fill Up Your Heart (p. 74)

Notes from Our Practice
Mindful eating was fun! We'll try it again at dinner. Resting with the dragonfly felt really peaceful. When I was still, I noticed how happy I felt.

Be Mindful of How You Feel

While your opening and closing routines may stay the same practice to practice, the main activities might reflect how your child is feeling when you come together to practice. Here are three scenarios with corresponding practice plans for inspiration.

Scenario #1

Luna has a band recital this evening and is feeling very nervous about it. She's having trouble focusing, and her thoughts keep drifting to "What if . . . ?"

Our Practice Plan

Date September 27   **Practice Time** 11 a.m.

Opening Routine
3 belly breaths (p. 36)
Check In (p. 101)

Our Practice
3-2-1 Focus (p. 51)
Counting Clouds (p. 69)
I Can Do It (p. 99)
My Peaceful Place (p. 93)

Closing Routine
Choose a breath card and take 3 breaths (p. 45)
Hug It Out (p. 78)

Notes from Our Practice
I still feel a little worried, but my body feels more relaxed now. I'll practice "I Can Do It" again right before the recital!

Sebastian is having a tough day. Something is bothering him, but he doesn't want to talk about it. Instead, he's been stomping around the house.

Our Practice Plan

Date October 20   **Practice Time** 5 p.m.

Opening Routine

Shake It Out (p. 67)

Our Practice

Squeeze and Release (p. 86)
Five-Count Breathe Out (p. 60)
Sigh It Out Loud (p. 65)
Catch the Good (p. 80)
Legs Up the Wall (p. 91)

Closing Routine

3 belly breaths (p. 36)
Check In (p. 101)

Notes from Our Practice

It felt so good to shake it out and sigh out loud, and I liked naming things I feel grateful for. I'm ready to talk about my day now.

Scenario #3

Amara told her parents that she has been feeling sad because their family will be moving to a different city soon. This practice is designed for her to have some supportive, quality time with a parent.

Our Practice Plan

Date _January 12_   **Practice Time** _2:45 p.m._

Opening Routine
3 belly breaths (p. 36)

Our Practice
Ocean Waves (p. 37)
Sprinkle Kindness (p. 79)
Sensory Walk (p. 105)

Closing Routine
Three Wishes (p. 75)
Hug It Out (p. 78)

Notes from Our Practice
Spending time together made us both feel better. It also felt good to get outside and take a walk! Sending wishes to others made me happy.

Reminder

Mindfulness won't make everything better. If one (or both) of you is in a bad mood, mindfulness won't instantly snap you out of it. What it will do is increase your self-awareness, so you'll recognize the feeling and not hold on to it so tightly. In the space of mindfulness, you acknowledge and accept the feeling, then make a decision about what to do next. You'll be in charge, not your emotions.

Your Mindful Day

Chapter 8, "Go," is all about you and your child taking your practice outside of the connection corner and into your day. Over time, adding quick mindfulness activities across your day will likely become second nature. Here's a sample of a mindful day. You can find the template on page 122.

Our Mindful Day

Morning
Sunrise Breathing (p. 98)
Make It Mindful—brushing teeth (p. 100)
Check In (p. 101)

Midmorning
3-2-1 Focus (p. 51)

Afternoon
Check In (p. 101)
4 p.m. Connection corner time!

Evening
Mindful Eating—first few bites of dinner (p. 49)
Fill Up Your Heart (p. 74)

Bedtime
Make It Mindful—brushing teeth (p. 100)
Winding Down (p. 92)
Mindful Breathing (p. 39)

Reflect to Connect

At the end of each connection corner session, or after each activity, you may want to take a few moments to reflect together. Many times, these discussions will occur naturally as you explore the activities.

One of the simplest, yet most impactful questions you can ask is: "What did you notice during that activity?" It's important to preface it by letting your child know that there are no wrong answers when it comes to mindfulness, only *your* answer. The goal is not necessarily to feel calm, but to be aware. Prompt them to notice any feelings, thoughts, and physical sensations that arose during the practice. For example, after a calming activity from chapter 7, "Rest," ask your child what their body feels like when they're relaxed versus tense. Be sure to let them know how it feels for you as well.

After certain activities, you may want to discuss how or when the strategy could be used in real-life situations, for example, when they get frustrated. Include your own examples in the discussion and, of course, model using the strategies in real time.

Note: You know your child best. If they ever seem uncomfortable with any of the activities, simply stop. Don't feel as though you should push through just because it's "supposed" to be calming.

Enjoy Your Practice

After all this formal setup to get your practice started, please don't forget the most important part: have fun! Mindfulness doesn't need to be serious. You and your child are learning valuable skills and helpful strategies, but the most important part is the time you're spending together and the connections you're making.

When I discovered mindfulness, I had no idea that it would completely change my life. I made it my mission to share it with as many people—of all ages—as possible. Getting the chance to share it with you and your child has been an honor. To me, mindfulness is the gift of presence and connection. This moment is all there really is—so why not be fully there? And if you're sharing this moment with one of your favorite people, all the better.

APPENDIX

Mindful Dragonfly (page 94)

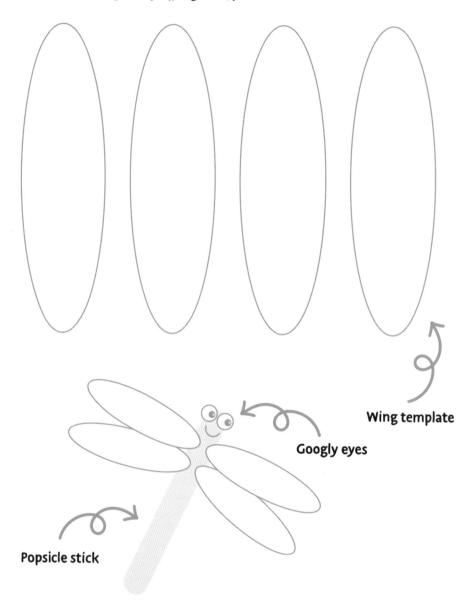

Wing template

Googly eyes

Popsicle stick

You can download the Mindful Dragonfly template at mindfulwithmebook.com

Our Practice Plan

Date .... Practice Time ....

Opening Routine

....

....

....

Our Practice

....

....

....

....

....

Closing Routine

....

....

....

Notes from Our Practice

....

....

....

You can download the Our Practice Plan template at mindfulwithmebook.com

Our Mindful Day

Morning

....
....
....

Midmorning

....
....

Afternoon

....
....
....

Evening

....
....
....

Bedtime

....
....
....

You can download the Our Mindful Day template at mindfulwithmebook.com

RESOURCES

Books for Children

* *Breathing Makes It Better*, by Christopher Willard and Wendy O'Leary. This book is a lovely reminder for all of us to pause and breathe when difficult feelings show up.

* *Here and Now*, by Julia Denos. A beautifully illustrated celebration of present moment awareness and connection.

* *I Am Peace: A Book of Mindfulness*, by Susan Verde. This book gently guides children through simple practices to feel present and peaceful. (Check out the entire *I Am* series.)

Books for Parents

* *Breathe, Mama, Breathe: 5-Minute Mindfulness for Busy Moms* and *Don't Forget to Breathe*, by Shonda Moralis. Filled with simple yet meaningful daily practices, these books help you find mindful moments even on the busiest of days.

* *Growing Up Mindful*, by Christopher Willard. For a deeper dive into sharing mindfulness with children, this book is a great resource for parents, therapists, and educators.

* *Wherever You Go, There You Are: Mindfulness Meditation in Everyday Life*, by Jon Kabat-Zinn. This accessible and relatable book helped deepen my own understanding of mindfulness as well as my practice.

References

Brown, K. W., & Ryan, R. M. (2003). The Benefits of Being Present: Mindfulness and Its Role in Psychological Well-Being. *Journal of Personality and Social Psychology, 84*(4), 822–848.

Flook, L., Smalley, S. L., Kitil, M. J., Galla, B. M., Kaiser-Greenland, S., Locke, J., Ishijima, E., & Kasari, C. (2010). Effects of Mindful Awareness Practices on Executive Functions in Elementary School Children. *Journal of Applied School Psychology, 26*(1), 70–95.

Kabat-Zinn, J., Lipworth, L., & Burney, R. (1985). The Clinical Use of Mindfulness Meditation for the Self-Regulation of Chronic Pain. *Journal of Behavioral Medicine, 8*, 163–190.

Schonert-Reichl, K. A., & Lawlor, M. S. (2010). The Effects of a Mindfulness-Based Education Program on Pre- and Early Adolescents' Well-Being and Social and Emotional Competence. *Mindfulness, 1*(3), 137–151.

Sciutto, M. J., Veres, D. A., Marinstein, T. L., Bailey, B. F., & Cehelyk, S. K. (2021). Effects of a School-Based Mindfulness Program for Young Children. *Journal of Child and Family Studies, 30*, 1516–1527.

Siegel, D. J., & Bryson, T. P. (2012). *The Whole-Brain Child.* New York: Random House.

Tang, Y. Y., Ma, Y., Wang, J., Fan, Y., Feng, S., Lu, Q., Yu, Q., ..., & Posner, M. I. (2007). Short-Term Meditation Training Improves Attention and Self-Regulation. *Proceedings of the National Academy of Sciences of the United States of America, 104*, 17152–17156.

Zelazo, P. D., & Lyons, K. E. (2012). The Potential Benefits of Mindfulness Training in Early Childhood: A Developmental Social Cognitive Neuroscience Perspective. *Child Development Perspectives, 6*(2), 154–160.

ACKNOWLEDGMENTS

I am exceedingly grateful to those of you who have inspired and supported me through the process of dreaming up, talking incessantly about, and finally writing this book. It's been quite a journey to this point, and there's a whole team of people I'd love to thank.

Foremost, thank you to my husband, Eric Tarnowski, for reading, editing, encouraging, listening, loving, being there, and always making me laugh. Mostly, thank you for believing in me.

Thank you to my wonderful, witty, and super-creative family: my parents, Anne and Fred; my siblings, Owen, Maureen, and Caitlin; my brother-in-law, Trevor; and the world's best nephew and niece, Jack and Isla. I'm grateful for your love and encouragement.

Natalie Garber Martin, your text from a few years ago, "Let's make a book," was a nudge I couldn't ignore. Hard to believe, but here we are! Thank you for your gorgeous art and for your support along the way.

A big thank you to my editor, Elizabeth Dougherty, for your encouragement, guidance, and wisdom. You have been a calm, steady presence throughout this entire process.

Much gratitude to the team at the Collective Book Studio, especially Angela Engel, Elisabeth Saake, AJ Hansen, and Rachel Lopez Metzger. Carole Chevalier, I'm in awe of your talent.

Kate Janeski, thank you for your thoughtful feedback and contributions; it means so much to me that you're a part of this.

Special thanks to Melanie Smith for holding open many of the doors that led me to my true path and ultimately to this book, and to Denise Veres for creating Shanthi Project, an organization that has positively impacted so many lives, including my own.

And to all the students I've had the privilege of working with through the years: thank you for being mindful with me.

Sarah Dennehy

About the Author

Photo: Danielle Gardner

Sarah Dennehy, M.Ed., began her mindfulness practice while working as a behavioral specialist one-on-one with parents and in schools. Seeking new effective ways to help young clients deal with stress and anxiety, Sarah earned teaching certifications for children's yoga and mindfulness. Sarah then founded The Mindful Space (createamindfulspace.com), which offers mindfulness training for kids, parents, teachers, and therapists. She's also a program director for a nonprofit that provides trauma-informed mindfulness in schools. Sarah lives in Eastern Pennsylvania with her husband, Eric.